LAST CHANCE TEXACO
and
PASTORAL

Two One-Act Plays

by
Peter Maloney

SAMUEL FRENCH, INC.
45 WEST 25TH STREET   NEW YORK 10010
7623 SUNSET BOULEVARD HOLLYWOOD 90046
LONDON   TORONTO

Copyright ©, 1985, by Peter Maloney

ALL RIGHTS RESERVED

CAUTION: Professionals and amateurs are hereby warned that LAST CHANCE TEXACO and PASTORAL are subject to royalties. They are fully protected under the copyright laws of the United States of America, the British Commonwealth, including Canada, and all other countries of the Copyright Union. All rights, including professional, amateur, motion pictures, recitation, lecturing, public reading, radio broadcasting, television, and the rights of translation into foreign languages are strictly reserved. In their present forms the plays are dedicated to the reading public only.

LAST CHANCE TEXACO and PASTORAL may be given stage presentation by amateurs upon payment of a royalty of Fifteen Dollars for the first performance, and Ten Dollars for each additional performance PER PLAY, payable one week before the date when the play(s) is/are given, to Samuel French, Inc., at 45 West 25th Street, New York, N.Y. 10010, or at 7623 Sunset Boulevard, Hollywood, CA. 90046, or to Samuel French (Canada), Ltd. 80 Richmond Street East, Toronto, Ontario, Canada M5C 1P1.

Royalty of the required amount must be paid whether the play(s) is/are presented for charity or gain and whether or not admission is charged.

Stock royalty quoted on application to Samuel French, Inc.

For all other rights than those stipulated above, apply to Writers & Artists Agency, 162 West 56th St., New York, N.Y. 10019.

Particular emphasis is laid on the question of amateur or professional readings, permission and terms for which must be secured in writing from Samuel French, Inc.

Copying from this book in whole or in part is strictly forbidden by law, and the right of performance is not transferable.

Whenever the play(s) is/are produced the following notice must appear on all programs, printing and advertising for the play(s): "Produced by special arrangement with Samuel French, Inc."

Due authorship credit must be given on all programs, printing and advertising for the play(s).

Anyone presenting the play shall not commit or authorize any act or omission by which the copyright of the play or the right to copyright same may be impaired.

No changes shall be made in the play for the purpose of your production unless authorized in writing.

The publication of this play does not imply that it is necessarily available for performance by amateurs or professionals. Amateurs and professionals considering a production are strongly advised in their own interests to apply to Samuel French, Inc., for consent before starting rehearsals, advertising, or booking a theatre or hall.

No part of this book may be reproduced, stored in a retrieval system, or transmitted in any form, by any means, including mechanical, electronic, photocopying, recording, or otherwise, without the prior written permission of the publisher.

ISBN 0 573 60062 7   Printed in U.S.A.

PASTORAL
or
Recollections of Country Life

A Comedy In One Act

by
Peter Maloney

for Kristin Griffith

PASTORAL
or
"Recollections of Country Life"
by
Peter Maloney

was first produced by
The Ensemble Studio Theatre
as part of
"MARATHON '83"
May 25th — June 12th, 1983
with the following cast

KATE .... Kristin Griffith
KEVIN .... Daniel Stern

DIRECTOR: John Schwab
Producer: Billy Hopkins
Scenic Design: Johniene Papandreas
Lighting Design: Geoffrey Dunbar
Costume Design: Deborah Shaw
Sound Design: Bruce Ellman
Stage Manager: Joan Ungaro

THE ENSEMBLE STUDIO THEATRE
Curt Dempster, Artistic Director; David S. Rosenak, Managing Director; Teresa Elwert, Production Manager; Richard Costabile, Production Stage Manager. Thanks to Actor James Ryan, who participated in an early reading of the play, and to Marvin Bakalar.

ACKNOWLEDGEMENTS

On Monday, May 2, 1983, *Pastoral* was read aloud for the first time in the offices of The Ensemble Studio Theatre. The play which opened three weeks later was very different from the version which was heard on that spring day. Without the incisive comments and questions of the director, John Schwab; without the polite refusal of the actors, Kristin Griffith and Daniel Stern, to ever be untrue to their characters and the dramatic situation in which they found themselves engaged; and without the constant and loving support of my friend and stage manager, Joan Ungaro, *Pastoral* would not exist in its present form. I wish to thank these artists for their good work and for their inventive contributions to the play.

There is a small farm in northwestern Connecticut, and *Pastoral* as a story would not exist were it not for the continued hospitality of the farm's owners, Meg and Larry Stone, and the continued hostility of their roosters. Horace was Meg and Larry's first rooster, and he would attack me and any other man with frightening irregularity. He didn't seem to mind the womenfolk. Horace was killed one night while defending his flock from some varmint or other, probably a fox.

Of course there was another, younger rooster ready and waiting to take his place, and this one, (so unlikeable that he was never even given a name), proved to have an even worse personality than Horace. Frank "Butch" Sherwood was the man who taught me how to stand my ground and defend myself against that vicious bird, but I was never very good at it and was always afraid of him. This rooster's downfall was that he would attack women as well as men, and it was feared that he would one day

ACKNOWLEDGEMENTS
(continued)

strike at Meg and Larry's fearless young daughter, Molly Ace. One day when Larry was away up north, Meg had to call Clayton "Skeet" Morey and ask him to come over and "put the rooster down" as they say in the country. Well, Skeet came over, and he put the rooster down all right, with one shot from his Winchester 22 Magnum. "He'd gaming blood in him," Skeet was heard to say at the burial.

Of course there was another rooster ready to take that nameless rooster's place. The current ruler of the roost is Horace's son, who, I'm pleased to say, for all his height and handsomeness, despite his regal bearing and his eagle eye, seems quite uninterested in humankind and lets me be. Thank you to the good people of Salisbury.

Finally, a thank you to The Ensemble Studio Theatre and its Artistic Director, Curt Dempster, for supporting my work and producing my plays.

CAST OF CHARACTERS

Kate
Kevin

TIME

Summer

PLACE

The country, another state

PASTORAL

SETTING: Small farmhouse porch and front yard. Three steps rise from the lawn to the porch. White pillars peeling paint. A screen door leading into the house. On the porch, a white-painted wicker chaise lounge and a wooden rocking chair. Several pillows of various sizes on the chaise lounge. A spreading pink geranium in a glazed ceramic bowl. A large portable tape-recorder/radio. In the yard in front of the porch, a wicker ottoman. As the house lights go to half and out, the ending of the second movement of Beethoven's Sixth Symphony is heard. In the dark, the "Shepherd's Song" on solo flute. The stage lights come up as the "song" is repeated. (Switch sound from house speakers to tape recorder speaker onstage.)

LIGHT: Mid-afternoon sun filtered through the leaves of large maples at the foot of the lawn. KATE sits, meditating in comfortable semi-lotus position, on the wicker ottoman. Her hands rest on her thighs, palms upturned. Her eyes are closed, a relaxed half-smile on her face. The second movement of the Sixth Symphony ends, the tape stops. KATE stays in position for a moment. Sound of birds chirping. KATE slowly opens her eyes, stretches like a dancer. She gets up, goes to the tape recorder on the porch. As she does so, from offstage right, a rooster is heard crowing. Then the sound of a man screaming, as if he is being attacked by a monstrous and frightening enemy. KATE turns to watch the unseen battle.

KEVIN. *(from offstage)* AGGHHH! Get away! GET AWAY!
KATE. Kevin! Don't run!
KEVIN. Back off! AGGHHH! Kate!
KATE. What?!
KEVIN. Help!

(KEVIN enters, brandishing a small log in one hand, waving a plastic bucket in the other. He wears large rubber boots over his baggy trousers.)

KATE. *(Grabs an old broom from the porch.)* Don't run! Remember what Meg said!
KEVIN. To hell with Meg!
KATE. Hey, that's my sister!
KEVIN. Where's the axe?! *(He runs behind the house, begins to hunt for the axe. Noises off.)*
KATE. *(Warily wielding the broom, keeps her eye on the unseen rooster.)* She said don't run. Just stand your ground.
KEVIN. *(from offstage)* Where's that axe? Kate!
KATE. What?
KEVIN. *(Comes from behind the house carrying a broad snow shovel, still carrying the small log.)* Where is he? I'm going to kill him. *(The rooster crows from offstage right.)* I'll kill you! *(He lurches toward the rooster, pulls back, hurls the small log offstege right, staggers back.)*
KATE. Good shot! You got him.

KEVIN. I got him. Is he dead?
KATE. Just stunned, I think.
KEVIN. Not dead?! Just stunned? *Where is that axe?* I'll finish this. *(He starts for the back of the house again.)*
KATE. *(Tries to restrain him.)* No, **Kevin!**
KEVIN. Yes! I want him dead!
KATE. He's not our rooster!
KEVIN. I don't care!
KATE. He's coming to.
KEVIN. What?
KATE. Stirring.
KEVIN. Stirring?! Jesus, God. *(He first picks up the wicker ottoman as if to use it as a shield, then drops it, runs up onto the porch, hides behind the chaise lounge.)* **Hide!**
KATE. I think he's done, for now. *(KEVIN has found a gardening claw behind the chaise lounge and holds it up, ready for anything as he watches the bird move from stage right toward stege left. KATE watches too, as she picks up the shovel which KEVIN dropped and puts the shovel and the broom against the porch railing.)* You held up your end very well. He may have new respect for you.
KEVIN. Respect! That's a laugh. He thinks he's won.
KATE. He may know it's a draw this time. *(From offstage (center) the sound of the rooster crowing triumphantly.)* **You're** right. He thinks he's won.
KEVIN. He's won again. I hate him. I hate him! I hate him! *I miss the city!* Let's go back.
KATE. We can't go back.
KEVIN. I'm not cut out for farming.
KATE. We said we'd stay.
KEVIN. We'll hire somebody else to do it.

KATE. It's our responsibility. *(The rooster crows again from offstage center)*

KEVIN. Shut up, you asshole!

KATE. Easy, Kevin. Calm down. You did good.

KEVIN. Good means dead. When he's dead at my feet, say good.

KATE. It's over now. Relax.

KEVIN. I can't relax while he's alive and running loose... Where is he, anyway?

KATE. He's gone.

KEVIN. He's probably getting laid right now, the bastard.

KATE. Fighting makes him feel sexy.

KEVIN. Fighting doesn't make you feel sexy. *Winning* a fight makes you feel sexy.

KATE. *(Goes to KEVIN, puts her arms around him from behind.)* I think you're sexy, even if you didn't win. Let's go upstairs.

KEVIN. What for?

KATE. What for?

KEVIN. *(breaking from her)* I've just had a very traumatic experience here.

KATE. I know you have. That's why you should come upstairs. It'll relax you.

KEVIN. I can't afford to relax. *(He looks warily around the yard.)* How come he never chases you?

KATE. I don't antagonize him like you do. Besides, I think he just hates men.

KEVIN. He couldn't hate me more than I hate him.

KATE. Hate's really not the word. I mean, *you* hate *him*, yes, but I don't really think he hates.

KEVIN. He's not intelligent enough.
KATE. Right. You're intelligent, therefore you hate. But Horace, he's too...
KEVIN. *(interrupting)* Bird-brained.
KATE. *And*, he doesn't have the time for hating. He's too busy, eating, sleeping, nailing all those hens of his, and mainly, keeping eyes out all the time.
KEVIN. For me.
KATE. For anyone or anything that threatens him.
KEVIN. How do I threaten......?
KATE. *(interrupting)* You just hit him with a log.
KEVIN. You're right.
KATE. What do you think he'll think the next time you come out, armed to the teeth?
KEVIN. I just protect myself is all.
KATE. A club in one hand, a snow shovel in the other, like a shield, big rubber boots.
KEVIN. A defensive stance. Purely defensive.
KATE. *(Moves down to the ottoman, sits, looks in her totebag for a tube of sun-screen lotion, speaking as she does so.)* All dressed up like Tweedledum, ready for a battle.
KEVIN. You laugh because you don't know what it's like to have him come at you, those big wings flapping...
KATE. *(interrupting)* "Just then flew down a monstrous crow and frightened them away."
KEVIN. What crow? I'm talking about Horace... where was I?
KATE. Big wings flapping.
KEVIN. Big wings, yeah, and feathers bristling, beady eyes blazing, and then, just before he strikes, he looks

into your very soul. *(KATE has been applying sun-screen to her nose while KEVIN has been imitating the rooster about to strike.)*
KATE. He does not.
KEVIN. Yes he does.
KATE. He doesn't look into your very soul.
KEVIN. He looks into mine!
KATE. He watches your feet! Meg told you that. *(She goes up onto the porch, grabs a pillow from the chaise lounge, sets it down on the edge of the porch and demonstrates a stand-off with the "rooster.")* She says ... just stand your ground ... and when he strikes ... BOOM. *(She kicks the pillow off the porch.)*
KEVIN. Meg's never been attacked by Horace. That rooster's got it in for *me*.
KATE. He's more than got it in for you, he's *got* you, Kevin. You know why? 'Cause he's prepared to die in order to protect his flock, or his honor, whatever it is. He's fully committed, and you aren't.
KEVIN. You're saying that rooster's more committed than I am?
KATE. Yes, in his way.
KEVIN. Well you're wrong. I am just as committed as he is.
KATE. Committed to what?
KEVIN. To what? ... Well, to you, for one thing.
KATE. You are?
KEVIN. Yes. I am. Are you?
KATE. Committed?
KEVIN. Yes.
KATE. *(A brief pause, after which she breaks away.)* What

does that *mean?*

KEVIN. You used the word. You brought it up.

KATE. I was talking about Horace.

KEVIN. You were talking about me. And I'm talking about you. Are you committed?

KATE. To you?

KEVIN. To me.

KATE. Yes.

KEVIN. Then why are we living in separate apartments?

KATE. *(Breaks away from him again, goes down steps to her tote bag.)* Let's not get into that again.

KEVIN. Why not?

KATE. 'Cause I don't want to, that's why not.

KEVIN. Okay... Will you think about it?

KATE. Please don't push me. *(She takes the New York Times from her tote bag, sits on the bottom porch step.)*

KEVIN. I'm not pushing, I'm just asking... Will you think about it the next time you're meditating?

KATE. *(laughing)* You don't think while you're meditating.

KEVIN. *(Sits near her on the steps.)* You don't?

KATE. That's the whole point about meditating. Not to think of anything.

KEVIN. I didn't know that... So what good is it? I mean if it doesn't lead you to some kind of...

KATE. What?

KEVIN. I don't know.... Kate, listen, if you're really committed to me.

KATE. Yes?

KEVIN. If you really love me...

KATE. I do.
KEVIN. Tell me your mantra.
KATE. No!
KEVIN. *(not a question)* There's only *one*, isn't there.
KATE. You can't tell someone your mantra.
KEVIN. Only one mantra in the whole world.
KATE. If you tell it...
KEVIN. *(interrupting)* If you tell it, you'll find out it's the only one.
KATE. It loses its *potency!*
KEVIN. And they're selling this one little mantra...
KATE. *(interrupting)* Kevin!
KEVIN. To *millions* of people...
KATE. God!
KEVIN. For *millions* of dollars.
KATE. That is the most ... *cynical* thing I've ever heard.
KEVIN. I know. I'm sorry. Look, Kate. I know how much your mantra means to you. Your meditation ... gives you something, I don't know... It gives you something I don't have.
KATE. You can learn to meditate.
KEVIN. I don't want to meditate! That's not the point. I'm saying you retreat from me.
KATE. No I don't.
KEVIN. You do. You're always meditating.
KATE. No I'm not.
KEVIN. Or taking walks, alone, or *reading*. You read more than anyone I know.
KATE. I like to read.
KEVIN. I know you do, but that's another thing you do

by yourself. Like the other night, when you came over? We were supposed to spend the night together? So after supper we watched the news...

KATE. *Together.*

KEVIN. Yes, but that's not fun. We watched the news and got depressed together, then you went into the other room to read and left me sitting there.

KATE. I'm sorry, Kevin, I don't like the Muppets.

KEVIN. It's my favorite show.

KATE. Did I say you shouldn't watch it?

KEVIN. It's got to do with sharing.

KATE. But later I suggested Scrabble and you wouldn't play.

KEVIN. You cheat at Scrabble.

KATE. I do not cheat! Is it my fault I have the O.E.D. and you're still using that tattered dictionary you used in college?

KEVIN. You keep getting off the point. I want to be with you and you keep leaving me.

KATE. You're *here* with me. I *brought* you here. Because I *want* you here.

KEVIN. I *hate* it here! *(KATE in her frustration shoves KEVIN, who falls over onto the porch. She moves down to the ottoman.)* To say we'd run a *farm* for *two weeks.* Jeez, we must've been insane.

KATE. My sister's been real good to us.

KEVIN. I know she has.

KATE. We've got a weekend country place, and we don't have to pay.

KEVIN. We're paying now.

KATE. Their first vacation in three years.

KEVIN. I didn't know it'd be like this. Up at six to feed the chickens, slop the pig ...... milk the goats.

KATE. You just aren't used to it.

KEVIN. I'll never get used to it. Besides, what good's that milk?

KATE. It's better for you.

KEVIN. Tastes like goat.

KATE. It's better than the store-bought kind.

KEVIN. Yeah well, I'd rather drink that milk than shop in town, have people look at us that way.

KATE. What way?

KEVIN. You know. As if we don't belong up here.

KATE. We don't belong up here.

KEVIN. Like we came from some foreign country, just dropped in from outer space.

KATE. We're visitors.

KEVIN. Will you stop being reasonable! This is America! Land of the free!

KATE. Home of the brave.

KEVIN. Yeah! You don't need passports here to go from state to state! Haven't these people heard of the melting pot?

KATE. I don't think so.

KEVIN. We've shopped in that store every weekend for a year, you'd think by now...

KATE. *(interrupting)* It's the territorial imperative. Ardrey says...

KEVIN. *(interrupting)* Please don't quote Ardrey at me, *please!* That pseudo-scientist!

KATE. His hypothesis is very attractive.

KEVIN. I know all about his hypothesis. You know

what he did before he became a pseudo-scientist?

KATE. Before he became an *anthropologist.*

KEVIN. He was a playwright!

KATE. So?

KEVIN. He makes things up! *(He sits in the rocking chair on the porch.)*

KATE. *(Comes up to him.)* All right, forget Ardrey. Look at your own experience. When you first came to the city, you told me the kids on your stoop wouldn't speak to you, they wouldn't even look at you, you had to squeeze through that gang every day to get to your front door?

KEVIN. Yeah?

KATE. But when some guys from another neighborhood made a move on you one night, what happened?

KEVIN. I know, I know...

KATE. The gang on your stoop jumped up and chased 'em off the block, right? It just takes time.

KEVIN. That was different. Those kids were Puerto-Ricans. These people are New Englanders. They look at me like, I don't know...

KATE. They look at you the way they look at any city person on their turf.

KEVIN. How do they know I'm from...

KATE. *(interrupting)* They know. They know you're not from here. You don't have a gun-rack in the window of your pick-up.

KEVIN. I don't have a pick-up.

KATE. There you go. Your car's too clean, the back seat's not all full of junk. No sticker on your windshield for the dump. A million things that say "just passing through, I'm only here on weekends."

Kevin. On *weekends*, that's another thing I just found out. They raise the prices weekends at the store! Once Sunday's gone the "special" signs go up, and it's bargain city for the local yokels. Burns me up.

Kate. How do you think they feel when they come to the city?

Kevin. Why do you take their side?

Kate. I'm not taking anybody's side. I just want you to see things in perspective.

Kevin. I see things in perspective. Here's the country, there's the city, I'll take the city.

Kate. I like it here.

Kevin. I can't sleep here. It's too noisy.

Kate. I sleep fine here.

Kevin. You sleep good anywhere.

Kate. Unless *you* wake me up. Hollering out the window at three in the morning. At the *insects! (She moves away from KEVIN, sits on the chaise lounge.)*

Kevin. I've never heard such a racket in my life. I mean, I remember crickets. I heard one, once. It was nice. But this... give me the sirens, the screams, the fighting neighbors. At least you can call the cops, bang on the walls, but *this, there's no dealing with it!*

Kate. Kevin, you can't keep getting angry at people and things all the time.

Kevin. Why not?

Kate. 'Cause it's not good for you, that's why not. Look at what happens between you and Horace.

Kevin. Not everyone can be as calm as you! You take things as they come. Whatever happens, that's all right with you. You sit under a tree to read, the Gypsy moths start shitting on your book...

KATE. *(interrupting)* They're caterpillars.

KEVIN. What?

KATE. They aren't moths yet, they're caterpillars.

KEVIN. See what I mean? You *know* them, like they're friends of yours. Okay, the Gypsy *caterpillars* start shitting on your book, you just get up and move onto the porch. *I* hear those little bastards munching away, devouring every leaf, and shitting on me at the same time, I wanta rev up the chain saw and cut the fucking tree down!

KATE. See what I mean? You cherish your anger, you nurture it. It's gonna kill you someday Kevin. You've got to settle down. Find your center. Decide what you want and go for it.

KEVIN. I told you what I want.

KATE. What do you want that you can *have*, that's possible, that's not out of the question?

KEVIN. Like a Coke? ..... Okay, okay... This is what I want.

KATE. Yes?

KEVIN. I want to go back to the city.

KATE. You can't go back. You...

KEVIN. *(interrupting)* Promised, I know.

KATE. Next Tuesday you can go back.

KEVIN. Next Tuesday, that's so far away.

KATE. But while you're here, what do you want?

KEVIN. I ... don't want to get chased by that bird again.

KATE. All right. That's a start. It's a negative start, but it's a start.

KEVIN. I said it wrong. I *want* ... to ... not get chased by that bird again.

KATE. *(laughing)* And how are you going to get what you want?

KEVIN. By keeping him locked up.

KATE. Now that's not fair.

KEVIN. At sunset, they go in to roost, we shut the henhouse door and keep it shut.

KATE. Kevin...

KEVIN. For the rest of the time we're here.

KATE. It's good for them to exercise.

KEVIN. To *exercise?!*

KATE. They lay better, Meg says.

KEVIN. To chase me around the yard? Scare me to death?

KATE. *(picking up a book)* It also says right here...

KEVIN. Right where?

KATE. The Woman's Guide...

KEVIN. *(interrupting) That* book.

KATE. To Country Life and Husbandry.

KEVIN. I read that book.

KATE. You did?

KEVIN. *(crossing to her)* Read in it. Read enough to know it's written by some dyke.

KATE. What?

KEVIN. Lesbians! Look here. *(He takes book from KATE, leafs through it.)* The people here think I'm so strange...

KATE. I can't believe you read that book and that's what you got out of it.

KEVIN. There's weirdos in the country, too. I'll find it, just a second...

KATE. What difference does it make in any case? Who cares if she's a lesbian or not?

KEVIN. Listen to this: "I think it was while I was building the breeding barn that David's true feelings came to the surface. When David saw me, a woman, erecting a strong, practical, yes, beautiful structure, which rose higher each day in the corner of the field we had selected for the purpose, something inside him died."

KATE. *(trying to get book back)* Stop it Kevin, this is ridiculous.

KEVIN. *(evading her, flipping pages)* "The day the breeding barn was finished, David left."

KATE. Kevin, I have no interest whatever in building a breeding barn.

KEVIN. *(flipping pages)* The plot thickens.

KATE. Or anything else for that matter.

KEVIN. "It is a constant source of wonder to me how comfortable I feel with *Sarah*. She simply *understands*, by some mysterious process which I cannot begin to fathom; and without the constant analysis and argument which, looking back, seems to have characterized my relationship with David...

KATE. *(interrupting)* Are you afraid I'm going to leave you?

KEVIN. *(a beat)* And all the other men with whom I've shared large portions of my life."

KATE. Kevin...

KEVIN. *And* ... on page ... ninety-seven: "Sarah has moved in! Today we castrated all the young he-goats. *It was hard and bloody work."*

KATE. Of course it was!

KEVIN. Of course it was? Of *course* it was?! How would you know? You've never done it! You've never castrated a goat! This is your sister's farm, not yours. I'll bet *she's* never castrated a goat. You don't live here, these aren't your problems, Kate! *(He throws the book down on the chaise lounge, goes down the porch steps and into the yard.)* You *read* about them, you hear Meg *talk* about them, and you think it's *great!* Some great adventure, yeah, with blood and sweat and death! You want to live up here? You want to homestead in the wild?

KATE. Maybe.

KEVIN. *Maybe?* You're living in a dream world, Kate!

KATE. Are you through?

KEVIN. *Dream world!*

KATE. Are you *through?!* 'Cause if you are, why don't you just go in the house and call the drug store, ask them when's the next bus out!

KEVIN. I might just do that.

KATE. Pack your bag and you get on that bus and get back to the city!

KEVIN. Good idea!

KATE. You really kill me. Jesus, you are arrogant. And childish, that's the worst of it. You haven't stopped your whining since we hit the West Side Drive!

KEVIN. I'll stop right now!

KATE. Nobody dragged you here!

KEVIN. *You* dragged me here!

KATE. Go get the bus!

KEVIN. I'll hitch!

KATE. Who'd pick you up?!

KEVIN. I'll *walk!*

KATE. You'll have to. Who'd pick up a clown! A fool! That's all you are. You make me laugh, you're good for that.

KEVIN. *(Starts to go off right.)* I'm going.

KATE. *(Starts to go off left.)* Go!

KEVIN. *(turning back)* But let me tell you this: You'll never make it here.

KATE. *(turning back)* You mean without you? Ha! *(KATE and KEVIN now face each other across the yard, the small porch separating them.)*

KEVIN. 'Cause you can't be the *center* here.

KATE. I don't need you.

KEVIN. Everything doesn't revolve around *you* here. 'Cause no matter what costume you put on, nature....

KATE. *(interrupting)* What costume?

KEVIN. Your 'Country Woman' costume; your 'Superwoman' costume; your whole 'blissed-out meditator' act!... *(He kicks the wicker ottoman.)* Nature doesn't care. About *anything*, let alone *you!*

KATE. *(Goes up the porch steps to screen door.)* Get out of here.

KEVIN. NATURE DOESN'T CARE!

KATE. *(going into house, slamming screen)* WHO CARES?!

KEVIN. I CARE!

KATE. *(returning)* Yeah well, you care too much.

KEVIN. Too much?

KATE. It makes me nervous.

KEVIN. How could I...?

KATE. *(interrupting)* Since we got here, I don't know, it's different.

KEVIN. Yes, we've lived together for a week!

KATE. I just know things were good before. I don't want that to change.

KEVIN. What are you scared of?!

KATE. I'm not scared!

KEVIN. Then open up!

KATE. I'm open!

KEVIN. Not to me, you're not!

KATE. I'm open to the *moment*, not the *future*, God you talk about forever!

KEVIN. Who said forever? I'm talking about *now*.

KATE. Now is *now*. *This second here!*

KEVIN. You're right! It's gone.

KATE. What?

KEVIN. That second's gone.

KATE. I...

KEVIN. *(looking and pointing)* There goes one. Here comes another, there it goes.

KATE. Kevin...

KEVIN. They're speedy little devils, aren't they? Look out! Duck! *(As He points, KATE turns to look and ducks.)*

KATE. Stop!...

KEVIN. There's no stopping them. That's the thing about seconds. *(He tries to "catch" seconds, missing each time. He looks as if he's trying to catch flying insects, his head swivelling around as he snatches at them and misses them.)* Time marches on ... and there's nothing we can do about it. *(He slaps a "second" which has landed on his neck, looks at his hand.)* Missed. *(He spots a "second" across the yard, makes his way toward it, bending down to try to grab it.)* Oh! There's a *beautiful* moment. Time flies, when you're having ... ugghhh. *(He *pretends to have strained his back in reaching for the "second", looks like an old man when he tries to straighten up.)* We're gettin' old, Kate. Where has the time gone? Huh? Kate? Katie? Where are ya, darlin'? *(Playing the old man, he is now nearly blind. He looks around for KATE, grasps the porch railing in his shaking hand and starts shakily for the steps.)* Oh, there you are. And just as beautiful as ever. *(He manages to mount the steps, approaching KATE who has been watching him with growing amusement. He extends his hand to her.)* How about a big ... wet one? *(KATE starts to extend her hand to him, but she is too late and KEVIN falls to his knees on the porch.)* Thanks ... for the memories. *(He falls forward onto the porch, reaches his hand up to KATE, who takes it. With one last shudder, he "dies.")*

KATE. Don't leave.
KEVIN. I won't. I didn't want to leave.
KATE. I know. I didn't want you to.
KEVIN. I know.
KATE. *(helping him to a sitting position)* We'll stay?
KEVIN. We'll stay. 'Til when?
KATE. 'Til Tuesday.
KEVIN. God.... Hey, we'll have fun! A good time, yeah!
KATE. *(laughing)* You don't mean it.
KEVIN. Yes I do. I'll ... mow the lawn! Work up a sweat, and then I'll ... split some wood, Oh Boy! ... What do you want to do? *(He gets up from porch steps, gets wicker ottoman, sets it in position on the ground.)* You want to meditate? *(KATE smiles. He goes up onto porch, picks up her book.)* You want to read? *(He puts his arms around KATE, looks up toward the bedroom window.)* You want to ... relax?
KATE. I don't know what I'm going to do. I don't like

making plans. Let's say I'll try to be more open ... to the possibilities.

KEVIN. Like moving in with me?

KATE. I'll think about it. *(She turns her head and she and KEVIN kiss. Smiling, she pulls away from KEVIN. She starts to go off the porch while KEVIN tries to pull her to the screen door. He gets the screen door open just as she, laughing, breaks away.)* I'll be right back. *(She runs offstage left.)*

KEVIN. *(Left alone, he bangs the screen door against his head twice, then once more. He lets the door close, looks around the yard, the porch. He picks up a pillow from the chaise lounge, looks at it, imagining that it is the rooster. He "strangles" the pillow, then beats it several times on the edge of the chaise lounge. He walks to the edge of the porch, sets the pillow down, backs off from it, watches it as if it were the rooster, then suddenly drop-kicks it into the yard. He goes into the yard, retrieves the pillow and tosses it onto the porch. He looks at the wicker ottoman, decides to try to meditate.)* Kate! What are you doing? Huh? *(He sits on the ottoman. Sound of birds chirping. He tries to get into the full lotus position. It is an incredibly painful process. He does as well as he can, gets as close to a lotus as possible, but is in pain as he closes his eyes and places his hands palms-up on his knees. KATE comes from off left carrying a burlap feed sack and an axe. She places the sack in KEVIN's left hand. He opens his eyes.)* What's this?

KATE. It's Horace.

KEVIN. Horace! *(He jumps up, holding the sack. Something inside the sack flutters once, just for a moment, then stops. KEVIN is frightened, but is afraid to drop the bag.)*

KATE. Careful. The bag's not tied.

KEVIN. Jesus, Kate.

KATE. And here's the axe.

KEVIN. What for?
KATE. To kill him.
KEVIN. Kill him?
KATE. You said you wanted to.
KEVIN. I know, but...
KATE. *(interrupting)* You should know, though, there's another rooster waiting to take his place. He doesn't act much like a rooster. He doesn't even *look* much like a rooster now, but if something were to happen to Horace....
KEVIN. *(He stands for a moment, the sack in one hand, the axe in the other, then he leans the axe up against the porch.)* I'm going to let old Horace go.
KATE. Okay. If that's what you really want.
KEVIN. It is.
KATE. Okay.
KEVIN. Okay.... Right here? Just open the sack?
KATE. Wherever.
KEVIN. Right. Hey, he might like it better over there. Across the road. In those high weeds.
KATE. He might. *(KEVIN starts to go off right. KATE goes up the steps onto the porch, pushes "play" button on the tape-recorder.)*
KEVIN. *(Calls from offstage.)* Hey, Kate!
KATE. What?
KEVIN. What happens when I open up the sack?
KATE. I don't know.
KEVIN. Dear God. Here goes...

(The sound of the rooster crowing is heard.)

KEVIN. Fly away. Fly away! Get away! Agggghhhhh! *KATE!*

(The rooster crows again as KEVIN screams from offstage as he did at the top of the play and the third movement of Beethoven's Sixth Symphony is heard coming from the tape-recorder. KATE, smiling, leans on the porch railing and watches the offstage battle as the lights fade.)

THE END

PROPERTY PLOT

ONSTAGE:
an old wooden rocking chair
an old wicker chaise lounge
   on which are several pillows of various sizes
a wicker ottoman
a pink geranium plant
a large portable tape-recorder/radio
a tape cassette
an old broom
a small pronged gardening tool
an oversized paperback book, a country scene on the cover, with title in large letters "The Woman's Guide to Country Life and Husbandry"
a tote bag (from local PBS station, with logo) containing: "Bain de Soleil" sunscreen lotion and a copy of the daily New York Times.

OFFSTAGE:
a small log (KEVIN)
a dirty plastic bucket (KEVIN)
a broad aluminum snow shovel (KEVIN)
a burlap bag, weighted (KATE)
an axe (KATE)

COSTUME PLOT

KATE:
light shirt
jeans
sneakers

KEVIN:
baggy painter's pants
big rubber boots with the tops rolled down
an old T-shirt
a hooded red sweatshirt

SOUND PLOT

1. Beethoven's Sixth Symphony (end of the second movement)
2. Sound of birds chirping
3. Rooster crowing (six or seven times during the course of the play)
4. Beethoven's Sixth Symphony (beginning of the fourth movement) (See note below)
5. Beethoven's Sixth Symphony (third movement "a merry gathering of country people") for curtain calls

NOTE: It was my original intention to use the beginning of the fourth movement of Beethoven's Sixth Symphony (the "Thunderstorm" movement) to punctuate the action during the attack of the rooster at the beginning of the play. The whirlwind music interrupted by the percussive "thunderclaps" would, I thought, be edited on tape to time out with Kevin's cries for help and would accompany the battle until Kate turned off the recorder. For various reasons, this idea was not realized in production. It may, in fact, be just a good idea which is impossible to realize on the stage.

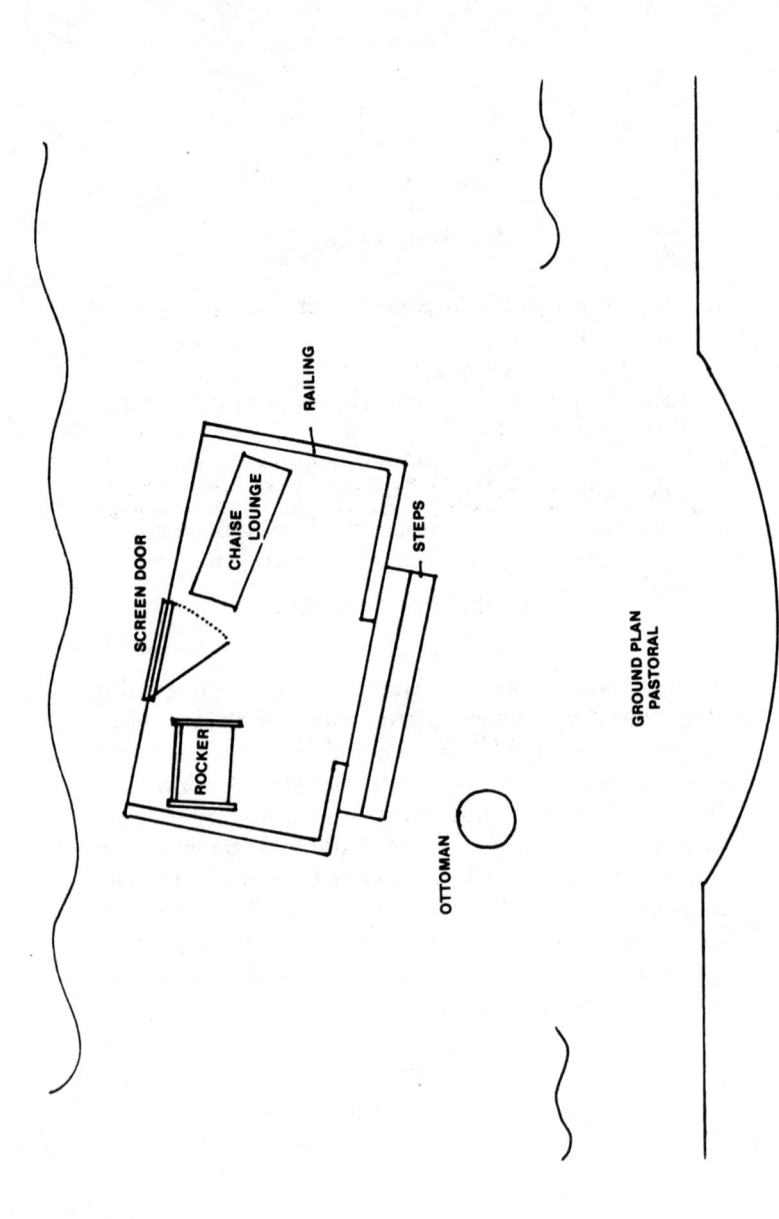

LAST CHANCE TEXACO

A Play In One Act

by
Peter Maloney

for Kristin Griffith

LAST CHANCE TEXACO

by

Peter Maloney

was first produced by
The Ensemble Studio Theatre
under the title *American Garage*
as part of

"MARATHON '81"

June 11th — June 20th, 1981
with the following cast

CISSY .... Kristin Griffith
RUTH .... Christine Jansen
VERNA .... Delphi Harrington

DIRECTOR: Stephen Zuckerman
Producer: Pamela Berlin
Scenic Design: Dale Jordan & Leslie Taylor
Lighting Design: Richard Lund
Costume Design: Elena Pellicciaro
Sound Design: Leslie Moore
Music by David Maloney
Stage Manager: Richard Heeger

THE ENSEMBLE STUDIO THEATRE

Curt Dempster, Artistic Director; Deborah Dahl, Managing Director; Brian Martin, Resident Scenic Designer; Randy Hartwig, Production Supervisor; Leslie B. Goldstein and Billy Hopkins, Associate Producers "Marathon '81"; Thanks to Actress Lois Smith, who participated in an early reading of the play, and to Joan Ungaro, Chris Moyer and Marvin Bakalar.

LAST CHANCE TEXACO
(American Garage)

was further developed at
Pilgrim Theatre's
THE ASPEN PLAYWRIGHTS CONFERENCE
Aspen, Colorado
William Shorr, Producing Director
William Gibson, Playwright in Residence
July 20 — 21, 1981
with the following cast

CISSY	Kristin Griffith
RUTH	Christine Jansen
VERNA	Lois Smith

DIRECTOR: Alice Spivak
Stage Manager: Karen Collins
Music by David Maloney

Thank you to Director Alice Spivak for her perceptive work on the acting text, and to William Gibson for his encouragement and advice.

LAST CHANCE TEXACO
(American Garage)

was produced by
The PEOPLE'S LIGHT AND THEATRE COMPANY
Danny S. Fruchter, Producing Director
as part of their
Second Annual New Play Festival
July 9th — August 8th, 1982
with the following cast

CISSY	Ceal Phelan
RUTH	Sherry Steiner
VERNA	Alda Cortese

DIRECTOR: Ernest Schier
Scenic Design: Norman B. Dodge, Jr.
Lighting Design: Adrienne Riemer
Costume Design: Lisa Hemphill-Burns
Music by David Maloney
Production Stage Managers: Linda Harris
and Katherine Pierce
Assistant Director: Sandy Dietrich

INTRODUCTION

Last Chance Texaco tells the story of three women in desperate need; of how, despite themselves, they finally come to each other's aid. It is a story of crime and punishment, of sin and redemption. The play is set in a green land on the edge of a desert, and it is anchored, even as its modern-day characters are, in the Old Testament.

There were a number of influences which led to my writing this play: A comment made by Edith Oliver, that good critic, urging writers of one-act plays to tackle weightier subjects .... Time lived in East Texas in 1966, working in the little towns of Denton County. Their names still echo in my memory like a litany: Venus and Maypearl, Midlothian and Red Oak, Pilot Point and Ponder. It was my first time west of Buffalo, New York ... A haunting poem by James Dickey inspired me .... John Lennon had just been killed at the time the writing began ... And underlying all is my interest in, and concern about what seems to be our American penchant for violence, the deep well of dissatisfaction and helplessness from which it flows.

CAST OF CHARACTERS

Ruth
Verna
Cissy

TIME

February, 1977, around 9 pm

PLACE

The American Garage; a small town in East Texas

LAST CHANCE TEXACO

SETTING: A corner of the American Garage and auto-repair shop. The place is dirty and dim, the only color a dark enamel green painted halfway up the walls. Industrial lights hang from the ceiling. Against one wall a long workbench cluttered with tools and toolboxes, thick repair manuals and parts catalogs. Above the workbench, a large section of industrial-type windows. Many of the panes are broken, and those that remain are dark and dirty. Also on the workbench: a radio, an old "Mr. Coffee" machine with a full pot of coffee ready, a portable tape recorder and a motorcycle helmet on which has been painted the name "CISSY." On the wall above the workbench are several color posters of motorcycles, including one which features a Harley-Davidson bike; a large calendar showing the month of January, 1977. The picture on the calendar is of a large-breasted pin-up girl in a bathing suit. The bathing suit is printed separately on a plastic overlay, and when the overlay is lifted, the girl is revealed in the nude. Also on the wall above the workbench: a telephone and an old intercom box with push-buttons, a roll of paper towels in a holder. High up on the wall, a stuffed deer's head, a six-point buck. Up two cement steps, a door leads into the attached house (offstage), a screen door separating the two spaces. A light switch is on the wall beside the door. A small refrigerator sits against the wall.

The playing space is basically an open one, the dirty floor is clear, but scattered around are empty oil drums, a pile of old tires. Furniture consists of a captain's chair held together by wire, a wooden stool at the workbench, and an old Dodge truck seat sitting on the floor. A pillow and blanket lie on the truck seat, Cissy's guitar leans up against it, and a cheap fibreboard guitar case lies open on the floor. Some feet away from the truck seat is an old heater, its cord trailing away to a socket in the wall. Fastened into the ceiling is a winch system from which a heavy iron hook hangs down above the center of the room. The large overhead door leading into the garage (which has within it a smaller door for easy entrance and exit), is not seen, but is heard operating from offstage right.

LIGHT: The lights in the garage are off. The only light in the room comes from the upper windows of the garage door, offstage right, through which a streetlight shines; from inside the house, shining through the curtained window in the door; and from the electric heater which is glowing in the dark. One might, viewing this set, empty of actors and in this light, be put in mind of a cave lived in by early humankind, lit by a dying fire.

Country music is heard coming from the radio. The house lights dim to half and go out as the music rises in volume. As the stage lights come up, the music goes down to a low level. We hear the sound of a tow-truck approaching, stopping. The motor is shut off and two truck doors open and close. As the door within the garage door opens, we hear CISSY's voice from offstage.

Cissy. You get yourself warmed up. I just wanta look at this under the light. *(We hear the sound of the door closing.)*

(RUTH enters the dark garage, slowly making her way toward the center of the room. Her foot hits something on the floor, the sound of metal clattering as it skitters across the concrete. RUTH gets to the center of the room, sees the heavy hook hanging down from its chain. Suddenly VERNA's voice, loud and sharp, comes from the intercom speaker.)

Verna. Cissy?!
Ruth. *(Startled, she jumps.)* Jesus.
Verna. Cissy?! I know you stole the coffee! I heard you takin' it, think you're so smart! *(RUTH glances around, finally placing the voice as coming from the intercom speaker.)* I know you're out there, now you answer me! *(After a moment, a brighter light goes on inside the house, VERNA comes to the door, opens it fast.)* You answer when I call you, girl!

(The light from the house shines into the garage through the screen door, backlighting VERNA, a once-attractive woman in her early forties. Her hair is disheveled and she is wrapped in an old chenile bathrobe over jeans and shabby slippers. Even in her present state of disarray, traces of her former beauty can be seen. VERNA peers into the garage, sees RUTH standing there. She opens the screen door, reaches out and flips the light switch on the wall. Harsh work light now shines on RUTH, a woman in her early thirties, dark and handsome. She wears a raincoat, dresses fashionably but not richly, and her black curly hair is covered by a felt beret. She is not

dressed for the weather and shivers in the cold.)

VERNA. Who're you?
RUTH. Uh...
VERNA. *(interrupting)* What d'you want?
RUTH. My car broke down. It's just a flat tire, actually.
VERNA. We're closed.
RUTH. I don't know how to change a tire.... I know that sounds stupid, but I just never had to. I just never learned. I was going to try, though, but the thing is... *(VERNA turns out the lights.)* the spare tire was flat too, so...
VERNA. *(interrupting)* We're closed. *(VERNA lets the screen door slam, slams the inner door as she goes back inside the house.)*
RUTH. *(Continues speaking in the same tone, looking at the closed door.)* So I just rode on the rim 'til I got to what's probably the only phonebooth in this godforsaken town... *(Still standing in the center of the garage, she looks around her.)*

(A dog is heard barking in the distance.)

RUTH. Huh... How many people does it take to make a town? ...Town, village ... *hamlet.* Maybe it's a hamlet. A hamlet on the moon. *(Suddenly, RUTH feels pain in her abdomen. She winces, her hands made into fists move to her belly, she moans quietly. The pain stops, she recovers.)*

(The sound of the door opening offstage. CISSY enters the garage,

rolling a flat tire in front of her. She is in her early twenties, and wears western boots and well-worn jeans, a loose olive-drab army jacket over a light shirt, and leather work gloves. Her long hair is in a braid.)

CISSY. You standin' around in the dark? Here, let's get some light on the subject. *(Drops the tire, crosses to the light switch, turns on the lights, turns, sees RUTH as if for the first time.)* I couldn't tell what you looked like in the dark out there. You're beautiful.

RUTH. I don't feel very beautiful. I've been driving for.... *(She is hit by the pain again, and her body tenses as she tries not to give in to it.)* days. *(She faints, starts to fall.)*

CISSY. *(Rushes to RUTH, catches her just as she collapses to the floor.)* Hey.... You alright?

RUTH. I fainted.

CISSY. Yeah.

RUTH. I'm sorry.

CISSY. Nothin' to be sorry about, you just fainted. We better get you sittin' down. *(She helps RUTH up and over to the truck seat. RUTH sits.)* There... You just sit.

RUTH. Thanks.

CISSY. How 'bout a cup of coffee? *(Heads for the workbench, turns off the radio, starts to pour a mug of coffee for RUTH.)*

RUTH. *(Tries to stand, sits back down.)* Would you hand me my purse? I've got some pills.

CISSY. *(Crosses to the center of the floor where RUTH dropped her purse, picks it up, hands it to RUTH.)* You aren't going to faint again, are you?

RUTH. I don't think so. I've just got ... cramps.

CISSY. Should you be drivin' 'cross country, hurtin' like that?

RUTH. I had to get away.

CISSY. You got a beautiful car there.

RUTH. It's a nice car.

CISSY. Beautiful. The Germans make good cars.

RUTH. Yes, they do.

CISSY. Expensive, though.

RUTH. Yes. It was a present. From my father.

CISSY. Your daddy must love you a lot.

RUTH. Yes, he does.

CISSY. He must also have a lot of money.

RUTH. Yes, he does.

CISSY. Are you Jewish?

RUTH. *(laughs)* Yes.

CISSY. *(Smiles, goes back to workbench, finishes filling mug of coffee, turns her head toward RUTH)* We had one here once, for about three weeks.

RUTH. Huh?

CISSY. Waiting for a part. A car like yours.

RUTH. Oh.

CISSY. I never met a Jewish person before. I never even saw one. You take cream or sugar?

RUTH. Cream, please.

CISSY. *(opening big jar)* All I got's this Cremora.

RUTH. Black will be fine.

CISSY. *(Capping jar, heads for door.)* No, you like cream, I'll get some.

RUTH. That's okay.

CISSY. We got milk, at least, inside, I'll...

RUTH. *(interrupting)* No, *Cissy. (CISSY turns, looks at*

RUTH *from the door.)* Black will be just fine. Please don't go in.

Cissy. Okay, if you're sure. *(Walks back to the workbench, picks up mug of coffee, hands it to RUTH.)*

RUTH. *(Takes two pills.)* Thanks.... Am I really in Texas?

Cissy. Sure are. *(Walks over to the flat tire, begins to inspect it.)*

RUTH. I thought it'd be warmer.

Cissy. Here, let me move this closer. *(Moves the glowing heater closer to RUTH.)*

RUTH. It's so good to rest. To not be driving. I kept waiting for the desert.

Cissy. You want west Texas. Cold there too, though. Snow.

RUTH. Snow?

Cissy. Six inches in Odessa yesterday.

RUTH. Odessa?

Cissy. Aunt Ceil says Butch an' Bobby made 'em a snowman right in the front yard.

RUTH. A snowman in Texas.

Cissy. West Texas.

RUTH. Jesus. *(CISSY turns, looks at RUTH (who is not looking at CISSY), then goes back to work.)* Is this unusual?

Cissy. Is what unusual?

RUTH. For it to be so cold.

Cissy. Nope. Six inches in Odessa's unusual, but we got all kinds of weather. It's a big state.

RUTH. *(casually)* Alaska's bigger.

Cissy. So I've heard.... How come you're so smart to know Alaska's bigger 'n then come down here expectin' sunshine 'n oranges in Denton County in January?

RUTH. *(pause)* It's February.

CISSY. Is it?

RUTH. *(Looks at her expensive watch.)* Seventh.

CISSY. *(flat)* You got a watch that says the date.

RUTH. *(a beat)* I'm sorry. I don't know anything about Alaska, or Texas either, for that matter. Geography's always been my worst subject.... I am heading toward California, aren't I?

CISSY. Yup. *(Begins to gather the equipment which she will use to repair the flat tire. She drags a galvanized metal tub from the side of the workbench toward center stage. She pulls a compressed air hose into position as well as a rubber hose connected to a water source.)*

RUTH. I hoped it would be warmer.... I'm tired of the cold.

CISSY. So New York got too cold for you an' here you are. Freezin' your butt.

RUTH. How did you know I'm from New York?

CISSY. How'd you know my name is Cissy?

RUTH. ....A little bird told me.

CISSY. That's funny. Ha. That's what Michael says. When he knows somethin' about me that I never told him.

RUTH. He does.

CISSY. Yeah. But he says what they tell him's nothin' compared to what he tells them. Michael talks to the birds. I wrote a song about that.

RUTH. You're a songwriter.

CISSY. Sure. I wrote eighty-seven songs. So far.

RUTH. That's a lot of songs.

CISSY. Yeah. I sent some to this publishing place advertised in this magazine, but I never heard from 'em. There's a lot of money in the song-writing business though, Michael says.

RUTH. Michael's your boyfriend?

CISSY. Yeah. He rides a Harley, just like that one. *(She points to a large photo-poster on the wall, goes to it, grabs several snapshots which are taped next to the poster, shows them to RUTH.)* There's Michael. That's his trailer. He lives out at Scheffler's Park.... There's Michael on his bike. That's me on the back. I take a terrible picture.

RUTH. No you don't.... You look happy.

CISSY. Yeah. You gotta be careful or you'll burn your leg on the exhaust. *(RUTH hands the photos back to CISSY, who goes to the workbench, tapes them back up on the wall.)*

RUTH. Michael rides a motorcycle and talks to the birds.

CISSY. Yeah.... He does tricks, too. He taught me one. You wanta see?

RUTH. Sure.

CISSY. Got a quarter? *(RUTH opens her purse, takes a quarter from her change-purse, hands it to CISSY, who has taken off her work gloves.)* Okay, now you see it... *(Takes the quarter from her right hand into her left hand. She holds her closed left hand up in front of RUTH, then slowly opens her fingers one by one. The quarter is gone.)* Now you don't.... Pretty good, huh?

RUTH. It's in your other hand. *(CISSY slowly opens the fingers of her right hand to show a metal washer. She hands the washer to RUTH, who is delighted.)* A washer! How did you do that?!

CISSY. You should see Michael. He can do things. I

saw this trick on television? You know that young guy? Curly hair and teeth?

RUTH. I know the one you mean ... uh...

CISSY. *(interrupting)* Anyway, he's on this motorcycle. A Honda CB seven-fifty, and he rides it across the stage and up this ramp onto a platform surrounded by a kind of net? Well, the platform rises up into the air, and he's waving to the audience, and all of a sudden the net falls down and he's gone! The CB seven-fifty too, just vanished in thin air! Michael says he knows how the guy did it. Wouldn't tell me, though. Magicians never tell.

RUTH. Where's my quarter?

CISSY. *(delighted with herself)* There. It changed into a washer. Ha. *(RUTH looks at the washer, smiles. CISSY watches her.)* You married?

RUTH. No.

(VERNA's voice is heard over the intercom speaker.)

VERNA. Cissy!

CISSY. *(Stiffens, looks at RUTH, smiles.)* Some little bird. *(suddenly concerned)* Hey, how you goin' to pay for the tires? Can you pay cash? We don't take credit cards.

RUTH. How much will it be?

CISSY. Well, I can give you one new tire and you're on your way, but you really oughta let me give you a new spare or you'll get stuck again like now. A new steel-belted radial will cost you... *(She checks a large parts catalog on the workbench.)* forty-eight dollars, plus ten for the labor, five for the tow, plus tax'd be... *(Adds up figures on a pad.)*

RUTH. *(Opens her purse, checks for cash.)* You don't take *any* credit cards?

CISSY. We're barely open, got no gas to sell, we're out of business, practically. Another steel-belted'd be another forty-eight dollars, forget about the labor.

RUTH. How much would it be just to repair that tire?

CISSY. With the tow, and with the tax, that's ... hell, forget the tax, let's say twenty dollars even.

RUTH. *(counting cash)* Could I write you a check?

VERNA. *(over intercom)* CISSY!

CISSY. *(Slams a tool down hard on the workbench.)* SHIT! ....I need the cash. *(RUTH crosses up to CISSY, hands her two ten-dollar bills, which she puts in her pocket.)* Thanks. *(CISSY crosses to the flat tire and begins to work on the repair. She turns on the water and, using the hose, puts a small amount of water into the galvanized tub. She then picks up the air hose and fills the flat tire with air.)*

(VERNA enters at the beginning of this work. She opens the inner door, bends over, picks up a cardboard box full of things, pushes the screen door open, comes toward the outside door, stage right, not looking at RUTH. VERNA sees RUTH sitting on the truck seat, but does not acknowledge her.)

VERNA. You couldn't answer, could you?

CISSY. Wouldn't.

VERNA. Wouldn't, then, you wouldn't answer. I'm so sick of this I'm 'bout to die.

CISSY. You're sick of it an' 'bout to die but it suits me just fine. I'm happy as I've been in years.

VERNA. You'll catch your death sleepin' out here.
CISSY. A lot you care.
VERNA. I care.
CISSY. I'm warm enough.
VERNA. You're warm enough.
CISSY. I'm *too* warm. *Hot.* I'm boilin' over, wish it'd get *colder!*
VERNA. Mary, Mary, quite contrary.
CISSY. That's right.
VERNA. *(Sets the box down stage right, near the outside door.)* Be contrary, then. See what it gets you.
CISSY. What's that?
VERNA. Things I'm gettin' rid of.
CISSY. His things?
VERNA. Hush!
CISSY. That's *his* things?
VERNA. Yes, your father's things.
CISSY. Not in here, you don't.
VERNA. It's my house, Cissy.
CISSY. You can have the house. The garage is mine an' I don't want his stuff in here.
VERNA. Well I don't want it in the house.
CISSY. Well put it outside, then.
VERNA. *(Crosses off and out toward the garage door as RUTH lights a cigarette with her Dunhill lighter. We hear the door within the garage door open, close, then VERNA returns from off right.)* I'll put it out tomorrow. Freezin' out.
CISSY. Now. Put it outside *now.* I don't want it in here.
VERNA. Well put it out yourself, then.
CISSY. I won't touch his stuff!

VERNA. Then don't touch mine!

CISSY. I don't want anything of yours.

VERNA. You took the coffee! Tried to be so quiet, but I heard. Think you're so smart. *(CISSY turns away from VERNA, picks up the inflated tire, lowers it into the tub of water.)* Can I have a cup? *(CISSY stops work, sighs.)* Please? *(CISSY goes to the workbench, pours a mug of coffee, sets it on a corner of the workbench, goes back to work on the tire. She slowly rotates the tire in the tub, carefully inspecting the wet, exposed portion of the tire for air bubbles which will indicate a puncture. VERNA crosses to the workbench, picks up the mug of coffee, sips.)* Thanks.... Good coffee.... What you doin'?

CISSY. This lady got a flat.

VERNA. Oh. *(VERNA looks at RUTH. Smiles.)* I'm Verna. Cissy's mother.

RUTH. I'm Ruth.

VERNA. Ruth. Is that your car outside?

RUTH. Yes.

VERNA. Nice car.

CISSY. It was a present from her father.

VERNA. That's nice. Well, Ruth, the garage is closed, but Cissy's good at fixin' tires. We had to close, you know. Skilled labor's hard to find, and a garage without no one can do the work's like a.... what? *(Looks at RUTH as if she expects her to supply the missing simile.)*

RUTH. Uh ... I don't know.

VERNA. Hmm. Well, I don't know either, and that's the truth. I just don't know.

CISSY. Anymore.

VERNA. Anymore.

(The sound of a motorcycle is heard, approaching the garage. CISSY stops work, listening, waiting, her back to RUTH and VERNA. VERNA watches CISSY. The sound gets louder as the motorcycle nears the garage, gears are shifted and the blare of the exhaust is very loud as the bike passes, then the sound diminishes. CISSY, who has stood up, now kneels again and goes back to work. She sees her mother watching her.)

CISSY. That was Jimmy Harrelson.
VERNA. You still think he's comin' back.
CISSY. That was a BMW!
VERNA. Humph. All sound the same to me.
CISSY. All sound the same to you.
VERNA. Loud. Rude. Like some huge ... animal, passin' wind.
CISSY. God!
VERNA. Don't you blaspheme. *(Crosses to the door.)* Thanks for the coffee. *(She opens the screen door, turns to RUTH.)* We don't take credit cards. *(She goes inside, closes the door. CISSY goes back to work, with energy, on the tire. Having located the puncture, she marks it on the tire with a yellow grease-pencil. She lifts the tire from the tub and wipes it dry with a dirty rag. Going to the workbench, she finds a roll of rubber cord and a special needle with which she will repair the punctured tire.)*

RUTH. It's amazing.
CISSY. What's amazing?
RUTH. Your knowing how to do that.
CISSY. This is nothin'. Michael taught me this. I wanted to learn everything, but Daddy wouldn't teach me. Taught my brother everything, an' Perry didn't even give

a damn about it all. Hell, I'm the one loved takin' things apart, rebuildin' 'em. Ha. Got a lickin' for it, more'n once. But, Perry got the learnin', taught him cars, trucks, tractors, all that. Shit, I'd a made a better mechanic than Perry any day of the week.
RUTH. Perry's...?
CISSY. Dead.
RUTH. Oh.
CISSY. Yeah.
RUTH. I'm sorry.
CISSY. Not as sorry as my daddy. He thought ol' Perry walked on water. But ... there's my daddy suddenly with nobody to help him. An' then he asks me to give him a hand here and there an' gettin' mad when I don't know. I told him, "You had your chance to teach me how, but it was always Perry." An' his eyes'd fill up when I said "Perry," but I didn't let that get me, oh I let him know. He'd just get mad, spout scripture at me, call me *loud*, an' *stubborn*, say *my feet abide not in my house*, I said I'm *here*, goddammit, what the hell you want?! He'd just get madder, still wouldn't teach me how. Anyway, then he hired Michael... *(CISSY looks over at RUTH, who has fallen asleep on the truck seat. She speaks more quietly.)* An' that's when the real trouble started. *(CISSY walks over to RUTH, covers her shoulders with the blanket lying over the back of the truck seat. As she does so, RUTH wakes, looks sleepily up at CISSY, who finishes covering her shoulders. CISSY smiles at RUTH, then picks up her guitar.)* This is the song I'm workin' on for Michael. *(She pulls the captain's chair out from the workbench, checks that the guitar's strings are in tune.)* Some of the lines I got from ol' hymns. *(She tunes a string.)* Song o' Solomon... *(She begins to*

play the guitar and sing her song.)
I KNOW A BOY, YOU CAN SAY HE'S A MAN,
BUT HE'S SOMETIMES JUST A BOY TO ME.
HE'S TALL AND HE'S TOUGH, HE CAN ACT AWFUL ROUGH,
BUT HE ALWAYS HOLDS ME TENDERLY.

IF I ONLY COULD MAKE YOU SEE
THAT MICHAEL, MY ANGEL, MEANS THE WORLD TO ME.
HE TALKS TO THE BIRDS, MY BELOVED, MY FRIEND.
HE'LL CARRY ME SOMEWHERE I'VE NEVER BEEN.

AS THE EAGLE SOARS HIGHER AND HIGHER ASCENDING,
AS THE RIVER FLOWS NEARER AND NEARER THE SEA,

(VERNA opens the door of the house as CISSY finishes her song.)

CISSY.
WE'LL FLY ON HIS WINGS AND OUR LOVE NEVERENDING,
THIS IS THE END OF OUR LOVE, TO BE FREE.
(RUTH has fallen asleep again.)

VERNA. *(Whispers, agitated.)* Cissy. I found somethin'. Look at this.

CISSY. Look at what? *(VERNA opens the screen door and enters the garage carrying a heavy object wrapped in an army blan-*

ket. CISSY sets her guitar down and crosses to meet her mother center stage. VERNA pulls the blanket away revealing a large artillery shell in its shiny brass casing. She stands holding it, cradling it in her arms.)

CISSY. *(Whispers, alarmed.)* What in hell is that?

VERNA. I don't *know*. It's a ... bullet.

CISSY. A bullet? For what kind of a *gun?*

VERNA. I don't *know.*

CISSY. That's not a bullet. Where'd you find it?

VERNA. In our bedroom closet.

CISSY. Your bedroom?

VERNA. Way back on the shelf.

CISSY. Put it down!

VERNA. *(She crosses to the boxes stage right, sets the shell down, begins to fold the blanket.)* It was all wrapped up.

CISSY. How long's it *been* there?

VERNA. God only knows. Maybe Harold brought it back with him from Korea.

CISSY. It's been up there for twenty years?

VERNA. More, maybe.

CISSY. In the house? All this time? What if it exploded?

VERNA. I don't know.

CISSY. How come you didn't know it was there?

VERNA. I never looked that close, I guess.

CISSY. You never cleaned that closet out before now?

VERNA. Of course I cleaned it.

CISSY. In twenty-five years?

VERNA. It was way up there, way back on the shelf.

CISSY. Your bedroom closet? We used to *play* in

that closet.

VERNA. Yes.

CISSY. Is that the only one?

VERNA. I hope so.

CISSY. I'm gonna go see.

VERNA. Will it be all right? To leave it there?

CISSY. Hasn't blown up in all this time, we prob'ly got a few minutes left. *(CISSY goes into the house, VERNA following.)* God!

VERNA. Don't blaspheme. *(VERNA lets the screen door slam. RUTH wakes up, looks around. She sees the shiny shell on the floor.)*

RUTH. Cissy? *(RUTH stands, looks around, walks over to the calendar, She reaches up and rips off the page which says January. She crumples the page into a ball. She notices the plastic overlay, lifts it up, revealing the large-breasted pin-up model, naked. She lowers the overlay, and the model once again wears her bathing suit. She lifts it again, looks, lowers it.)* Amazing.

CISSY. *(Comes from inside the house to the screen door.)* You call Casey! Tell him to stop foolin' around chasin' motorcycles, come over quick an' get it out of here! *(CISSY stands in the doorway, hollers back into the house.)* You're a lousy housekeeper! *(She enters the garage, letting the screen door slam.)* Been wantin' to tell her that for years. *(She crosses to the tire, goes back to work. During the following scene CISSY will thread the special needle with the rubber cord and plug the hole in the tire, cutting off the excess cord after doing so.)* I'm never havin' kids.

RUTH. Never say never.

CISSY. I mean it, what's the point? *(RUTH has another attack of pain, her hands clench into fists, go to her abdomen, she recovers.)* You know what works? For me, anyway? You'll prob'ly think this is crazy, but if you get yourself a green washcloth, it's gotta be *green*, an' you make a cup of camomile tea, real strong, an' real *hot*, then you soak the washcloth in the hot tea an' lay it across your stomach...

RUTH. *(interrupting)* I just had an abortion.

CISSY. *(She stares at RUTH. There is a pause.)* I don't believe in abortions.

RUTH. Neither do I.... I have terrible periods. Really bad cramps, awful... but, when I was late, I found myself praying, please let me bleed, *please...* *(There is a brief pause.)*

CISSY. *(Doesn't know what to say.)* I had a friend could suck blood right through the skin of her arm.

RUTH. *(thinking her own thoughts)* What?

CISSY. Yeah. That was her thing. *(CISSY lifts her wrist to her mouth, not demonstrating, but remembering.)* Must've had thin skin. That's what I figured. *(Looks at her wrist, then the other one.)*

RUTH. *(Walks around slowly, thinking it out. She has not spoken of this before.)* I thought I had it all together... My life was so... ordered. Everything in its place. And then, suddenly, there's this ... presence, inside you, disturbing all that order ... my life.

CISSY. I don't want kids, but if I had one, then I'd keep it, raise it up right. Michael, he wants kids.

RUTH. He sent me a check. No note or anything, just a check.

CISSY. Not even a note?

RUTH. For *half* the cost of the operation. Eighty-seven

dollars and fifty cents. I sent it back.

Cissy. Why'd you send it back? I'da kept it. He should pay half.

Ruth. I wanted more from him... I fantasized about doing something. Shooting him. Blowing up his factory.

Cissy. Good idea.

Ruth. Dynamite or something on the four corners of the building.

Cissy. That'd teach him.

Ruth. Yeah. But he's got all these people working for him... Besides, I wouldn't know where to get the dynamite. So, last ... Monday ... I went in, and that was that. It was easier than I thought it would be.

Cissy. Good.

Ruth. Yes. *(She wraps her arms around herself, lets something go which has long been held inside, cries.)*

Cissy. Ruth...

Ruth. I'm sorry... This is just a bad time, I guess.... After the operation, after I rested for awhile, I left the hospital and walked home through the park. It was cold, but the sun was shining. It was very bright. It was one of those days when every other person you see is crippled somehow, deformed. You ever been in New York?

Cissy. No. I'd like to see it, though.

Ruth. I knew I had to leave. I mean, I suppose those people might be perfectly happy, but... *(RUTH looks at CISSY for a moment, deciding whether or not to tell her something. CISSY, though a bit uncomfortable in the face of Ruth's story, is looking at her, waiting.)* The night before I left, I was in a restaurant with my parents. The waiter had just served us, and ... I felt something was wrong. I went downstairs, to the restroom, and I was hemorrhaging right there. It didn't hurt or anything, but there was a lot of blood, and I was so scared. I went upstairs and told my mother and father that I wasn't feeling very well, that I was going home. They said they'd leave too, and drive me home, but I said no, I'd rather go alone, so I quick kissed them goodbye and left them sitting there, got a cab to the hospital ... I might have been bleeding to death, and I couldn't tell them what was really wrong... I wanted to, but I just ... couldn't. *(RUTH has opened the crumpled calendar page which she has been holding in her fist. She looks at CISSY, who doesn't know to say, then at the calendar on the wall.)* That's some calendar.

CISSY. Ha. That's Michael just tormenting me. A girl with tits like that. He says he loves my little ones, but I catch him lifting up that overlay? He gets this smile on his face? Does this with his eyebrows. *(She raises her eyebrows up and down rapidly. RUTH starts to laugh, but ends up crying again.)* Oh, Ruth...

RUTH. Show me a magic trick, Cissy.

CISSY. I don't know any others besides that one.

(VERNA opens the screen door. CISSY turns back to her final work on the tire. Finishes plugging the leak and inflates the tire to its proper pressure during the following scene.)

VERNA. I can't get Casey on the phone. *(Crosses into the garage carrying yet another full cardboard box, looking at the shiny shell all the while. RUTH looks in her purse for something.)* May says he's up to Pilot Point. He's actin' in a movie.

CISSY. Actin'?

VERNA. They're shootin' movies up at Pilot Point. Casey's actin' the part of the Sheriff.

CISSY. Casey *is* the Sheriff.

VERNA. All I know's what May told me. She laughed an' said he's gonna be a movie star.

CISSY. A movie star? Ol' Casey? That'll be the day.

VERNA. That's what I told her. She just laughed.

CISSY. Where's Carlton, then?

VERNA. He's up there, too, directin' traffic.

CISSY. Directin' traffic, humph.

VERNA. Nobody mindin' the store.

CISSY. Be a good night to rob the bank. If we had a bank.

VERNA. *(She has set the latest box down stage right by the other boxes, and is staring at the artillery shell.)* You think maybe it's a missile?

CISSY. Huh?

VERNA. Your daddy worked the Nike missile base. 'Fore you were born, in Alvaredo, after he got back. I'm gonna call the firehouse, raise up Sy.

RUTH. Cissy? Have you got a kleenex, something? *(VERNA has headed for the wall-phone, turns to look at RUTH as CISSY takes a paper towel from the roll on the wall, hands it to RUTH.)*

VERNA. What's wrong with her?

CISSY. She's just upset.

VERNA. 'Bout what?

RUTH. It's nothing.

VERNA. She don't look too good.

CISSY. She's just not feelin' well.

VERNA. You sick?

RUTH. I just...
CISSY. *(interrupting)* She had an operation.
VERNA. Oh, poor thing, what was it?
CISSY. Leave her be.
VERNA. What is it? Tell me.
CISSY. You don't wanta know.
VERNA. Don't want to know? A woman's in my house an' cryin', tell me what is wrong!
CISSY. She just had an abortion.
VERNA. What?! *(Turns on RUTH. A command.) Get out of here!*
CISSY. Don't start on her!
VERNA. I don't believe in that an' won't have one who does under my roof.
CISSY. She doesn't care what you believe.
VERNA. I don't care if she cares or not.
RUTH. I don't believe...
VERNA. *(interrupting)* What you believe's your business, Miss, an' my belief's are mine. You married?
RUTH. No, but what's that got to do...
VERNA. *(interrupting)* Not married!
CISSY. So? What's marriage got to do with anything?
VERNA. What's marriage got to do? I married Harold, didn't I?
CISSY. You *had* to marry him!
VERNA. I did not have to marry him!
CISSY. Did too.
VERNA. Who told you that?
CISSY. Aunt Ceil did.
VERNA. Ceil's a busybody.

RUTH. Could you...

CISSY. *(interrupting)* Said you had to.

VERNA. Scandalmonger! Didn't *have* to. *Wanted* to. A man like that.

CISSY. Like what?

VERNA. Like Harold!

CISSY. Could we drop this, please?!

RUTH. A good idea.

VERNA. Stay out of this! And as for Ceil, she's proved herself to be what she has always been.

CISSY. What's that?

VERNA. You know. Don't have to say the word. Her boys told me.

CISSY. They told you what?

VERNA. Her men sleep over, stay the night!

CISSY. Good for Aunt Ceil!

VERNA. In Clayton's bed!

RUTH. Please!

CISSY. Clayton's gone! They are *divorced!*

VERNA. In front of those young boys!

CISSY. I doubt they do it right in front of Butch an' Bobby.

VERNA. Don't get smart with me. I know what I know.

CISSY. That's *all* you know.

VERNA. You think you know so much! A girl like you! When I was your age I was married, keepin' house, a baby at my breast, I had a *family!* You think there wasn't places I could go? To have it done? Across the tracks? You think I didn't know that others went there? In the night? Like Katie Rawls and others in that crowd? You think that I was dumb, a small-town country girl who didn't know? I knew. Answer me this: What would I have had if I'd had him cut out of me?

CISSY. What have you got?

VERNA. *(Slaps CISSY across the face with great force.)* What have I got?! You dare to ask me that? I'll tell you what I've got. I've got a son as dear in memory as he was when he was alive. I've got a house fallin' apart around my ears, a pile of bills to pay that's higher than the house. I've got a husband's left for somewhere, who I don't know if he'll be back or when, and a daughter who lives in the garage. *I went out full, and the Lord hath brought me home again empty,* but all that makes no difference, see. 'cause I've had what I've had, and I wouldn't have had any of it if I'd made that trip across the tracks twenty-five years ago. *(Turns to RUTH.)* So you get out of here, in your fancy foreign car your daddy gave you. Go on an' have your abortions whenever it's convenient, but just *get out of here.* *(Starts for the phone again just as RUTH speaks.)*

RUTH. Jesus.

VERNA. *(Wheels on RUTH.)* Jews killed Jesus!

RUTH. Jews killed...?

CISSY. *(interrupting)* Stop it!

VERNA. Look it up!

RUTH. Killed Jesus?! God!

VERNA. Don't you blaspheme! You're in my house!

CISSY. My house! The garage is mine!

VERNA. *I want her out of here!*

CISSY. She-is-a-*customer!*

VERNA. The garage is closed!

CISSY. I'm *workin'* on her *car!*

VERNA. Work on it then!

CISSY. *It's finished!* *(Lifts the tire from the floor and slams it down again. As VERNA crosses to the phone, CISSY whirls and shouts:)* Ruth! *(RUTH, who has collapsed on the truck seat, looks up at CISSY.)* You wanta see a trick?

RUTH. Yes.

CISSY. Okay. *(She goes into action. She takes off her gloves, then her fatigue jacket. VERNA starts to dial a number.)* You gotta help me, though. Be my assistant here, *do anything I say.* Okay?

RUTH. Okay.

CISSY. Okay. It's really what's called an "escape." You know Houdini? Michael's got this book about him, all his secrets printed in it. Houdini's great escapes exposed. *(Fishing around in the junk at the opposite end of the workbench from where her mother stands, CISSY has found a length of rope, which she hands to RUTH.)* Here. Tie my wrists real tight. *(She puts her wrists together, extends them abruptly toward RUTH.)*

VERNA. *(Stops dialing the phone, watches.)* What're you doin'?

CISSY. Tie my wrists real tight.

RUTH. *(Looks at CISSY's wrists, then up at her.)* You've done this before.

CISSY. *Just tie them.*

RUTH. All right. *(Starts to wrap the rope around CISSY's wrists.)*

CISSY. See, anything they put Houdini in, he could get out of. Make it tighter.... Good. Now tie it, make a knot.

VERNA. *(Hangs up the phone, still watching.)* Cissy.

CISSY. Now make another knot... That's good. I'm tied

up now, right? Can't get free?

RUTH. I don't suppose.

CISSY. Let's make it harder. Grab that hook up there.

VERNA. Don't do this. *(RUTH looks up at the hook hanging down from the chain-winch in the center of the ceiling.)*

CISSY. Just grab it, pull it down. *(RUTH stands, reaches for the hook.)*

VERNA. Cissy!

CISSY. Quiet! I need absolute quiet for this. *(RUTH pulls down the hook on its chain. It is very heavy in her hands.)* Now, put the hook through here. *(Extends her wrists.)* No, wait! My hair's not right. It should be down. Undo my braid. *(RUTH lets go of the hook, goes to CISSY, undoes her braid. CISSY shakes her head, her long hair falls free. She looks at her bound wrists.)* Ha. There's a statue in Dallas. In the museum there? Looks just like this. I really should be naked, Mama, shouldn't I.

VERNA. *(still upstage by the phone)* I don't know what you're talkin' 'bout.

CISSY. Don't you remember takin' us? How old were we? The man got mad at Perry, made you hold him back from climbin' that Egyptian temple.

VERNA. Don't remember.

CISSY. Sure you do. There was a statue there, in a courtyard, with green plants all around. It was called "The Captive Maiden." A beautiful girl, naked, with her wrists tied, standin' just like this. *(CISSY only has to extend her wrists slightly, lift her head slightly, to imitate the statue's pose. During the previous scene, and during the following scene, CISSY does not look at her mother who is upstage by the telephone and later by the door. She may direct a line now and then to VERNA, over her shoulder, but for the most part CISSY faces, and tells her story to RUTH.)*

VERNA. It was a colored girl. She was a slave. They were sellin' her.

CISSY. No, she was white.

VERNA. The *statue* was white. White marble. The girl was colored.

CISSY. No. It was a white girl, Mama. Captured by wild Indians. "The Captive Maiden." ...... Imagine this, Ruth. The maiden an' her lover. Lyin' there, on that ol' Dodge truck seat. They're lyin' there. under that blanket, all wrapped in each other's arms, just finished makin' love.

VERNA. Ha. Fornicating.

CISSY. Fucking, then.

VERNA. Don't say that word!

CISSY. Okay, then! *Makin' love.* By the light of that heater. They'd been real quiet *makin' love*, as quiet as could be, 'cause the maiden's mother's just inside the house asleep, or if she couldn't sleep, then watchin' some ol' movie on t.v., or readin' True Detective magazine.

VERNA. The Bible.

CISSY. Or the Bible. Lamentations, prob'ly. So, they were very quiet, even though that ol' Dodge seat groaned and echoed in the empty garage, an' they wanted to scream out, the maiden an' her lover, when the moment came, they screamed into each other's mouths, their voices rang inside each other's heads and sounded just like singin' under water.

VERNA. Cissy, please.

CISSY. And afterwards, they lay together in that heater's light, pretendin' it's a fire, imagining that they were somewhere else, I don't know where. And the maiden fell asleep in the arms of her lover, and dreamed she was flying, over the garage, the house, the town, everyone and everything she knew was down below and gettin' smaller by the minute. And then something went wrong with the flying, and she began to fall, down, fast, toward the house, the garage, she wanted to land on that truck seat so's not to be hurt after falling so far. And she did, she landed there, and she woke up. And the maiden was alone under the blanket, an' she thought maybe the lover too had been a dream, but she still held his leather jacket in her arms, was huggin' it. He'd been there, sure enough, but now was gone somewhere, had left her and the garage sometime before. There was a shadow standin' over her. Her father's shadow. In his hand he held a piece of rope. He hit her with the rope.

VERNA. Please don't.

CISSY. He hit her with the rope. She tried to stop him, but he was too strong. He hit her, thrashing, he was clumsy.

VERNA. He was drunk.

CISSY. Not drunk enough. The hitting with the rope wasn't enough. He grabbed the maiden's wrists and wound the rope around them, tied them tight. The maiden cried out loud for help but no one answered her. He hit now with his left hand, with his right he lifted up the captive maiden.

VERNA. God.

CISSY. Don't you blaspheme. He lifted up the captive

maiden from the Dodge truck seat. The blanket fell away and she was naked in the light from the heater. She was bleedin', too, from her lovemakin'. She'd never known a man before. She'd been suspected, warned, for years, but this one was the first an' only one. Her father saw the blood, an' dragged her cryin' 'cross the floor, the concrete scraped her feet, reached up... *(CISSY extends her bound wrists toward RUTH.)* An' now, the hook.

RUTH. *(quietly)* This is no trick. There's no escape from this.

CISSY. The hook.

VERNA. Don't do this, Ruth.

CISSY. You promised. Said you'd help. *(RUTH moves to the hook. She places the hook on the ropes binding CISSY's wrists. VERNA starts to move toward the door.)* Now, pull that chain.

VERNA. *(starting toward door)* Don't.

CISSY. Quiet! Watch! You'll see...

VERNA. Don't want to see!

CISSY. How this is done. Ruth, pull the chain. *(VERNA is at the door, but does not exit. RUTH moves to stage right, where the winch chain hangs down, and begins to pull the chain through the winch. CISSY's wrists are slowly pulled up, she has no choice but to give in to the force of the pulley system. At a point when CISSY's arms are above her head, when she is in a state of tension but with her feet still on the floor, RUTH stops pulling the chain. CISSY's speech begins when RUTH starts pulling the chain.)* See, she was bleedin', but that wasn't blood enough. He pulled the chain 'til she was hangin' there, an' thinkin' I was *born* to hang here in this garage, was *born* for this. She heard a sound she'd heard an hour before.

Belt buckle, this time Daddy's buckle, clink, behind her. She's screamin' bloody murder all this time, a noise to wake the dead!

VERNA. I didn't hear!

CISSY. But no one answered her or came.

VERNA. I didn't hear!

CISSY. An' then the leather whistlin' through the air an' strikin' flesh an' then the Bible started comin' out of him, he hollered like a prophet as he whipped her. Proverbs. Mother, give us one.

VERNA. I can't.

CISSY. You can, you know them all by heart. You taught me, Mama, please. I'm hangin' here, you can at least do somethin', please. Just shout it out, a proverb, *now!* "With hold not...

VERNA. *(Now standing at the top of the cement steps leading into the house, finishes CISSY's sentence without a break in the rhythm.)* Thy correction from the child, for if thou beatest him with the rod, he shall not die.

CISSY. That's good, but you don't have the rhythm right. He swung his belt, put everything, his whole weight into it, like this: Thou shalt *beat* him...

CISSY and VERNA. with the *rod* and shalt *deliver* his soul from *hell.*

CISSY. That's good, Mama. I thought I'd die, he hit so hard, hollerin' while he hit me an' screamin' all the while he called me *whore. Mama!*

VERNA. *(unable to resist CISSY's command)* A whore is a deep ditch and a strange woman is a narrow pit.

CISSY. And I screamed I'd lie in the deepest ditch for him, go down the narrowest of narrow pits *for him. Mama!*

VERNA. She lieth in wait for prey and increaseth the transgressors among men.

CISSY. And *yes,* I'd laid in wait for him *so long,* and we transgressed, and I don't care, and *yes,* I will transgress *again,* just let him come!

VERNA. He will come back.

CISSY. Oh Michael, *come to me,* I screamed and he kept hitting me, my father, Daddy don't! But he kept on 'til I was bleedin' now, for real, the blood ran down my legs and down that drain, I couldn't see, the hurt made everything turn red. And now *I'll beat the devil out of you* he said, so loud I thought the walls'd come tumblin' down, the whole town must've heard, *but no one came!*

VERNA. I didn't hear!

CISSY. You heard! You heard him shout that *in thy filthiness is lewdness and...*

VERNA. Because I've purged thee and thou wast not purged, thou shalt not be purged from thy filthiness anymore

CISSY and VERNA. *'til I have caused my fury to rest upon thee!"*

CISSY. Ezekiel! You heard!

VERNA. I heard!

CISSY. Ezekiel.

VERNA. *(giving in to the emotion finally)* Twenty-four-thirteen. I heard. I heard it all. My God.

CISSY. All right. Now let me down. *(RUTH starts for the chain.)* Not you, Ruth! Mother, let me down.

VERNA. *(crossing down to CISSY)* I'm sorry.

CISSY. It's too late for that. You should've come. You lay there in your bed and heard it all.

VERNA. I did.
CISSY. You should have come.
VERNA. I was afraid.
CISSY. That's no excuse. I needed you.
VERNA. I wanted to.
CISSY. You should have done.
VERNA. I know. I know I should have done. I was afraid. *(VERNA has removed the hook from the rope binding CISSY's wrists, then has collapsed onto the floor at CISSY's feet.)*
CISSY. *(Does not bend down to VERNA.)* I know you were, you've always been, but there's no need to be. I'm not a whore.
VERNA. I know you're not.
CISSY. I'm Cissy, standin' here. I love you.
VERNA. God knows I love you.
CISSY. I know you do. Get up, Mama. Stand up. *(VERNA, helped by CISSY, gets to her feet, embraces her daughter.)* Untie me now. *(VERNA starts to untie CISSY's wrists. After a moment, CISSY turns to speak to RUTH.)* Y'know, the thing about Houdini, it just killed me when I read that book of Michael's, the thing is, *he always had the key.* I mean people used to think he dematerialized or somethin', but that wasn't it at all. He always had the key.
VERNA. I'm sorry.
CISSY. Yes. I know you are.
RUTH. What happened then? What did your father do?
CISSY. He put his belt back on, and let me down, untied my wrists. And then I killed him.
VERNA. *(a beat)* That's not true.

Cissy. I'll kill him if he comes back here. I told him so as he went runnin' out, I said I'll kill you the first chance I get or I'll die tryin'! I said I am the pride of your heart who has deceived you and I will bring you down to the ground!

Verna. As thou hast done it shall be done unto thee.

Cissy. Thy reward shall return upon thine own head. And then he left. Nailed Michael's leather jacket to the door and went out huntin' him. *(RUTH turns to look in the direction of the garage door.)* An' neither of 'em's been back since. It's been two weeks.

Verna. Been fifteen days. I will not have him back.

Cissy. *(Turns upstage, moves to her jacket. Wounds on her back have opened and blood can be seen beginning to soak through her shirt.)* I'll kill him if he comes. 'less Michael comes back first.

Verna. He'll come.

Cissy. You think so?

Verna. Yes.

Cissy. I hope so, Mama. That's my only hope. *(Puts on her jacket and work gloves, crosses to the tire, rolls it across the floor and out stage right. Sound of the door opening, closing. There is a pause. RUTH is looking at VERNA.)*

Verna. *(Looks at RUTH, sees her as a person for the first time, speaks to her.)* She's leavin' home, I know it. Soon. He'll come back for her an' they'll go off. I had a dream about it, clear as a vision. He came back on his Harley before dawn, took her away with him down towards three-oh-eight. I didn't hear him come, but when they left the roar of that exhaust 'bout shook the house an' woke me up. I ran out after them an' tried to stop her leavin', hollerin' "Don't go," but they were fast, as fast as ... somethin', I don't know. I saw 'em from behind, him dressed in black, black jacket, black hair flyin', her behind him, naked, hangin' on, an' they were singin' somethin', couldn't hear the words, me runnin' in my bathrobe after them an' shoutin' "Please don't go." An' when they got to where McCausland forks, becomes the highway ... they *rose up* an' *left the road.* The dawn was comin' up an' they went with it, straight up in the air. I saw the chrome shine, Michael always kept his bike so nice, I saw the wheel spokes flashin' in the sun come up behind me, saw the wheels all spinnin' in the sun.... I walked back, all the neighbors had come out to see what's up. I showed them where the tire-tracks stopped, where they had left the road, gone off into the air. They all of them looked up with me. ...An' then we went on home.

(There is a pause, then the sound of the door opening off right.)

Cissy. *(Enters)* I think it's time you learned to change a tire.
Ruth. I think you're right. *(They both go out. Sound of door closing.)*
Verna. *(Left alone, she sits for a moment, looks at the hook hanging down from the ceiling.)* What sort of people are we, anyway? *(She sees the artillery shell on the floor, stands, goes to the wall phone, dials, waits for an answer, looking at the shell all the while.)* Sy? It's Verna. We got somethin' here.... I know it's late. I know, but I found somethin' in the closet... I don't know, I'm not sure *what* it is, it's big. An' shiny, looks like

it's a bomb... Well Harold left it, I don't know. It's somethin' from the war... He brought it home with him, I guess, though *why* God only knows... Real heavy, yes... It's maybe from the Nike base in Alvaredo... Get your clothes on, come an' see... No, Harold's left an Casey's makin' movies up at Pilot Point, May says... Get out here will you, get this off our hands, it's scarin' me to death. All right, we'll wait. *(VERNA hangs up the phone.)*

(The sound of the towtruck letting down RUTH's car is heard from off right. After a moment, CISSY comes in, tire iron in hand. RUTH follows, crosses to the truck seat to get her purse.)

CISSY. *(Goes to the cassette recorder on the workbench, removes a tape from the recorder, hands it to RUTH.)* Ruth, I want you to have this. It's a tape I made of some of my songs. Quality's prob'ly not too good, but...

RUTH. Thanks, Cissy.

CISSY. You sure you feel up to drivin'?

RUTH. Yes. I want to get there.

CISSY. *(a beat)* That's some stereo you got. How do you say that name?

RUTH. Blaupunkt.

CISSY. Blaupunkt.

RUTH. Well. Goodbye.

CISSY. Bye, Ruth.

RUTH. *(Brief pause. Looking at VERNA.)* Goodbye.

VERNA. You come on back now.

RUTH. Thank you. *(Starts for the door stage right.)*

CISSY. Stay warm.

RUTH. *(Turns, looks at CISSY, smiles.)* I'll try.

Cissy. Whole weather's changin' anyway. Very slowly. Mr. Kyle, he was my biology teacher? He said another ice age is comin' down. It's already happenin'. They used to call it the Bible belt, but now it's the Sun belt and everybody's comin' down. Won't they be surprised to see Butch an' Bobby's snowman on Aunt Ceil's front lawn. Ha.
Ruth. Goodbye.
Cissy. Goodbye. *(RUTH exits.)*

(Sound of door opening, closing. We hear RUTH's car start up and drive off. There is a pause. CISSY sits on the truck seat.)

Verna. Sy's comin' over, get that out of here.
Cissy. That's good.
Verna. She pay you?
Cissy. Yes.
Verna. Half's mine, by rights. *(CISSY takes the two ten-dollar bills out of her pocket, holds one out to VERNA, who comes to her, takes the money. CISSY picks up her guitar from beside the truck seat. A dog is heard barking in the distance.)* I gotta shop tomorrow. You need anything? *(CISSY shakes her head. VERNA heads for the door, opens the screen door, turns to CISSY.)* I'll get some coffee. *(CISSY turns her head to look at her mother. A beat. VERNA breaks the look, goes up the cement steps and into the house, shutting the screen door behind her and leaving the inner door open. CISSY turns front and strums her guitar as the lights fade.)*

THE END

PROPERTY PLOT

ONSTAGE:
a long workbench, cluttered with:
    tools and toolboxes
    thick repair manuals
    parts catalogs
    a radio
    a "Mr. Coffee" machine
    3 unmatched coffee mugs
    a portable tape recorder
    a tape cassette
    a motorcycle helmet with "CISSY" painted on it
    a large jar of CREMORA coffee whitener
    a battered spiral notebook containing Cissy's songs
    a notepad and pencil
    a length of rope

on the wall above workbench:
    a wall phone (dial type)
    a wall intercom box with pushbuttons
    a roll of paper towels in holder
    several large color posters of motorcycles
    a large color poster of a Harley-Davidson motorcycle

    several small photos of Michael, and Cissy and Michael on bike
    a large pin-up calendar with plastic overlay, showing month of January, 1977 (month of February, 1977 beneath)
    a stuffed deer head (six-point buck)

on the floor of the garage:
    an oil drum
    a pile of old tires
    a captain's chair held together by wire
    a wooden stool
    a Dodge truck seat
    a pillow and blanket (on the truck seat)
    an inexpensive guitar
    a fibreboard guitar case
    an old scoop-type electric heater (wired for lighting effect of glowing heater)

tools used for repairing tire, including:
    a hose with water source
    an air hose connected to compressed air source
    a galvanized metal tub to hold tire upright and in water
    a yellow grease pencil
    rubber cord used to plug puncture
    a special needle used to thread rubber cord into tire
    special cement used to secure rubber cord in tire
    knife or scissors to cut excess rubber cord from tire

    pocket gauge to check air pressure of tire
    (check with local garage to identify and obtain these tools)

a winch system with chain and hook (manually operated)

OFFSTAGE:
an expensive purse (RUTH), containing:
    small plastic pill bottle with pills
      wallet with paper money, including two ten-dollar bills and change purse with change including washer.
    a package of cigarettes
    a Dunhill-type expensive lighter
an expensive watch (RUTH)
a flat tire on its rim, from a BMW or Mercedes (CISSY)
a tire iron (CISSY)
several cardboard boxes filled with Harold's things (VERNA)
a large brass artillery shell (VERNA)
an army blanket (VERNA)

COSTUME PLOT

RUTH:
fashionable dress
fashionable raincoat
fine leather boots (not western)
felt beret

VERNA:
old jeans
wrinkled blouse
chenile bathrobe (preferably peach or pink, a neutral
  color)
shabby slippers

CISSY:
light shirt
well-worn jeans
western boots
olive-drab fatigue jacket (too big for her, the name
  FARLEY in black stenciled letters over breast pocket)
leather work gloves

SOUND PLOT

1. Country-Western pre-show music
2. Country-Western song from radio at top of play
3. Sound of tow-truck approaching, stopping
4. Sound of truck doors opening, closing
5. Sound of garage door opening, closing LIVE, off-stage right
6. Sound of Verna's voice over intercom LIVE from mike backstage
7. Sound of dog barking in distance.
8. Sound of motorcycle passing
9. Sound of tow-truck letting down Ruth's car
10. Sound of Ruth's car starting up, taking off
11. Sound of dog barking in distance

PRODUCTION NOTES

1.) *The Magic Trick:* Here is how Cissy accomplishes the coin trick. First of all, Ruth does not hand Cissy a quarter, she hands her a *washer*, which is in her change purse from the beginning. Cissy displays the washer to Ruth, being careful that the audience doesn't see it. With the washer in her right hand, parallel to the floor, she reaches to take it into her left hand. Her left thumb goes under the washer and her left fingers go over it. As they do so, she releases the pressure of her right fingers and the washer drops by its own weight into her right palm. She moves her left hand, closed as if holding a coin, up and to her left. The right hand drops naturally to her side, the washer "palmed" in that hand. As she lifts her left hand, her eyes follow that hand. Her right hand doesn't drop to her side until her left hand has risen to its final position. This must be practised by the actress until the move looks perfectly natural. The move of pretending to take the coin must look exactly as it would if she were really taking the coin. She should, in fact, repeatedly *really* take the coin into her left hand in order to see how her hands move while doing so, and her aim should be to move her hands in exactly the same way when only pretending to take the coin. It is the naturalness of the gestures and the actress' belief in what she is doing that will convince Ruth and the audience.

2.) About the artillery shell. The shell is an object of some power in this story and on the stage and is at the same time scary and funny. The audience will laugh when the blanket covering the shell is removed. They should laugh, but not too loudly or too much. If the shell is too large the laughter will be out of proportion and therefore undesirable. The shell should be large, but no larger than 17 inches tall and 4½ inches in diameter. It must look and feel heavy as it is a "live" shell which will have to be taken away by the police or fire department and exploded somewhere to render it harmless. It is not, however, a bomb, and it really will not explode if it is handled carefully. Somewhere in their consciousness the women know this, but it is still not the kind of thing which you want hanging around your house.

3.) About the calendar: You will probably have to make this up. It should be large enough to be seen clearly by the audience and the nude should be pretty and in a pin-up pose, certainly not the explicit sexual poses found in men's magazines today. Paint on acetate will do for the "bathing suit" overlay.

4.) The small refrigerator mentioned in the description of the setting is never used during the play and may be eliminated.

5.) Cissy's use of the exclamation "Ha." It is not really a laugh. Cissy uses it when she is pleased with herself, as when she has perceived something which no one around her has perceived. It is usually said without a smile.

*Music Copyright ©, 1985, by
Reilly And Maloney Music, BMI.
Used By Permission.

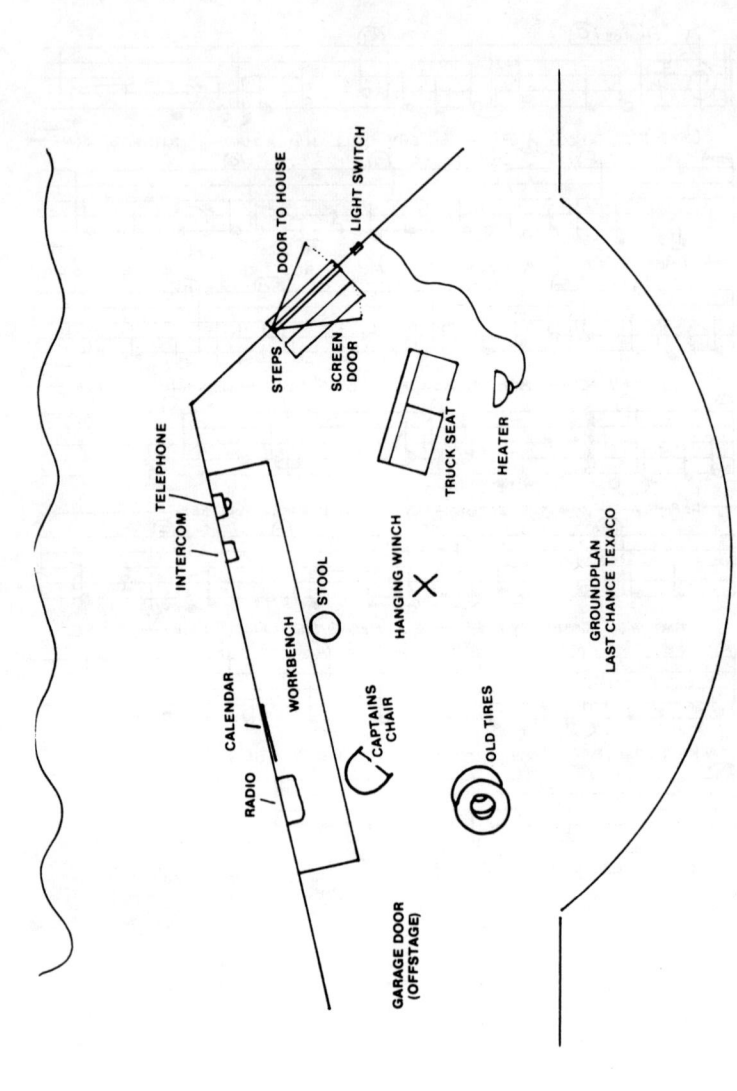

NEW ONE ACT PLAYS
from
SAMUEL FRENCH, INC.

APPROACHING LAVENDAR—AUTO-EROTIC
MISADVENTURE—BOX OFFICE—BUSINESSMAN'S
LUNCH—BUT NOT FOR ME—A CHANGE FROM
ROUTINE—CHEKHOV—CLOSET MADNESS—
CO-INCIDENCE—CROSSING THE BAR—THE DEVIL—
THE DICKS—THE DIVORCE—THE DOLPHIN
POSITION—DOSTOEVSKI—DREAMBOATS—
THE ENCHANTED MESA—FATHER AND SON—
FINE LINE—FORBIDDEN FRUIT—THE GIFT—GOD'S
SPIES—GOOD HELP IS HARD TO FIND—HERE
TO STAY—LAST CHANCE TEXACO—A LITTLE
SOMETHING FOR THE DUCKS—THE NECKLACE—
NOW DEPARTING—PASTORAL—PIECE FOR AN
AUDITION—P IS FOR PERFECT—THE RABBI AND
THE TOYOTA DEALER—RECEPTION—A SCENT
OF HONEYSUCKLE—SOMETHING TO EAT—
A TANTALIZING—THAT PIG MORIN—THURSDAY
IS MY DAY FOR CLEANING—WHAT WOULD
JEANNE MOREAU DO?

Consult our *Basic Catalogue of Plays* for details.

Other Publications for Your Interest

VIVIEN
(COMIC DRAMA)
By PERCY GRANGER

2 men, 1 woman—Unit set

Recently staged to acclaim at Lincoln Center, this lovely piece is about a young stage director who visits his long-lost father in a nursing home and takes him to see a production of "The Seagull" that he staged. Along the way, each reveals a substantial truth about himself, and the journey eventually reaches its zenith in a restaurant after the performance. "A revealing father-son portrait that gives additional certification to the author's position as a very original playwright."—N.Y. Times. "The dialogue has the accuracy of real people talking."—N.Y. Post.

(Royalty, $15-$10.)

LANDSCAPE WITH WAITRESS
(COMEDY)
By ROBERT PINE

1 man, 1 woman—Interior

Arthur Granger is an unsuccessful novelist who lives a Walter Mitty-like fantasy existence. Tonight, he is dining out in an Italian restaurant which seems to have only one waitress and one customer—himself. As Arthur selects his dinner he has fantasies of romantic conquest, which he confides to the audience and to his notebook. While Arthur's fantasies take him into far-fetched plots, the waitress acts out the various characters in his fantasy. Soon, Arthur is chattering and dreaming away at such a quick clip that neither he nor we can be entirely sure of his sanity. Arthur finishes his dinner and goes home, ending as he began—as a lover *manqué*. "... a landscape of the mind."—Other Stages. "... has moments of true originality and a bizarre sense of humor ... a devious and slightly demented half-hour of comedy."—N.Y. Times. Recently a hit at New York's excellent Ensemble Studio Theatre.

(Royalty, $15-$10.)